UNSTOPPABLE

Igniting the Power Within
*to **Achieve Your Greatest Potential***

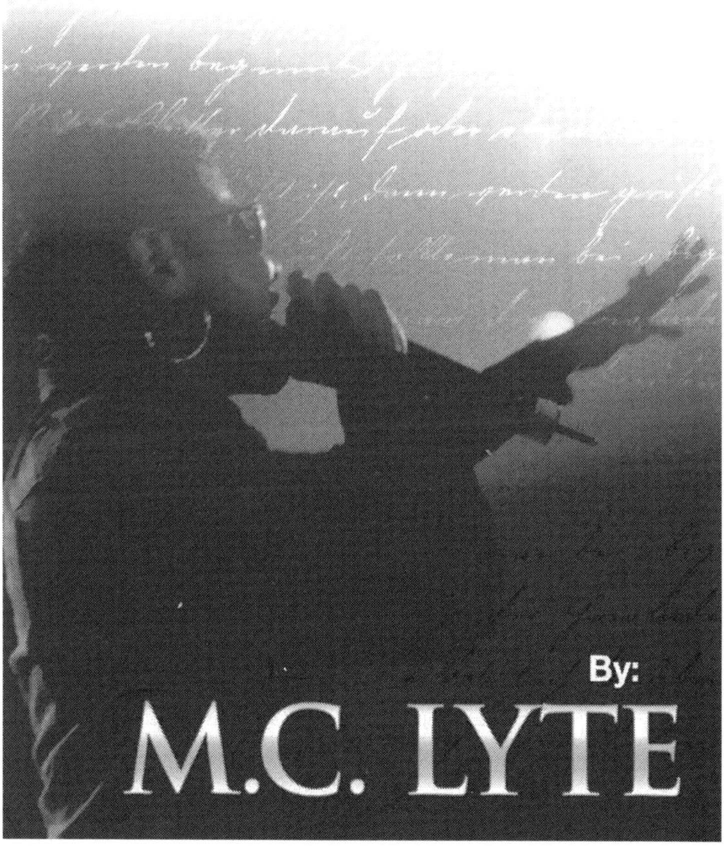

By:

M.C. LYTE

Publisher:	Sunni Gyrl, Inc.
Publisher Address:	14431 Ventura Blvd #120
Publisher City, State, Zip:	Sherman Oaks, CA 91423
Website:	www.mclytenow.com
Phone:	855.MCLYTE1
ISBN 13:	97809773232-8-9
Cover Design:	Daryl Bailey
Editor:	Lynn Richardson

This book is dedicated to Sunni and to all of my fans across the world who have shown me love continuously throughout the years. In this book, I have shared some of my inner most thoughts and hopefully you will become UNSTOPPABLE on your way to achieve all that God has in store for you.

MC LYTE

INTRODUCTION

Over the past few years and throughout my travels, I have been posed with the same line of questions from many, *"How do you remain relevant?"* and *"Why have you been able to stay in the business and others haven't?"* and *"What's the secret to still being here?"* or ***"Why do you seem to be unstoppable?"***

In all honesty, I attribute my long lasting career to a few things:

1. Knowing my overall goal is to inspire though whatever means God lies before me;

2. Remaining a student of life and being thankful for all of my experiences; and

3. Last but not least, the words in this book contribute to the code by which I have come to honor and live each and every day that God gives me another opportunity to interact in His world.

WHO ARE YOU?

Do you ever get this incredibly lonely feeling that no one understands you? Are you one of these people? Do you know who you are? The only way people will ever understand who you are is by you showing and telling.

However, if you do not know who you are, will they ever? Be certain and proud of who you are. Be you, no more, no less and only then will folks realize your uniqueness.

<u>YOU ARE . . . SIMPLY</u>

You are mighty.
You are beautiful.
You are self-sufficient.
You are tough.
You are great.
You are worthy.
You are amazing.

You are one of a kind and let no one tell you different.

GOD IS

*Life sometimes swallows you up and
leaves you blind.
Almost never coming close to the reason
as to why you were born.*

*But then all at once because you believed
God shines a light so incredibly bright
Down a path intended for your life
Showing yes
Life is a miracle
Yet some still take for granted
Because without God
There's no power to enhance it*

*You!
Move towards excellence even when
times are hard
Fear nothing
God is life and life is God*

YOU ARE SPECIAL
When are you going to get up and do the things you've always wanted to do but never made time for?

When will you reward yourself for all the hard work you've done over the years?

Get away, take a trip or do something you've never done.

Whatever you do, show yourself that you are special, because YOU ARE.

LIKE ATTRACTS LIKE

There is no guarantee that if you are nice, everyone will like you. You can bend over backwards to be cordial and you still stand the chance of not being accepted. If you believe you've got something special to offer, why spend valuable time trying to convince others? If you are not appreciated, move on and find someone who finds you worth discovering.

Give good energy. Like attracts like, with a positive attitude, you will draw others that are just as positive.

OPEN HEART

I am a firm believer in never doing anything that you don't want to do. But when it comes time for those rare exceptions, do it with a smile. Having a positive attitude while performing a task makes it all worthwhile. You may learn something new or better yet, help someone. You might teach someone or even like doing what you might have turned down.

Open heart, open mind . . . allows for endless possibilities.

LOVE IS

Love is so honest
It's either there or it isn't
Not by words but by action does one
determine whether he or she is loved
Love is not harming or alarming
Love is not beholding or controlling
Love is not the desire to have ownership
of some else's body
Love is not conditional or seasonal
Love is not tormenting nor mind blowing

Love is joyous and stupendous
Love is fulfilling and patient
Love is timeless and necessary
Love should be effortless
Love should be overwhelming like
roaring rapids
But calm like a soft tranquil brook
Love is in the heart
Love is God . . . Always

LIVING THE LIFE YOU WANT

There is absolutely nothing you can't accomplish in this life time. All things are possible if you believe and prepare for the moment you adamantly desire.

Look around and take note to those who are sitting dormant as the world swirls and time passes them by. Also, look at the few who are deemed successful due to all their stuff, items they worship and have become slaves to. NOW, look at those who are experiencing true happiness and living their best dream.

Living "The Life" is relative. What's most important is that you're content with the choices you've made and that HAPPINESS rules in "your life".

A REAL FRIEND

At a young age, friends mean everything. Our every moment goes toward wondering where they are, what are they doing and where are they going. So much time is spent keeping up with friends, but honestly, you will not see many of them in your adulthood.

If there are any friends worth keeping, it's the few who understand who you are, where you're going and want to help you get there. Real friends don't pressure you into behaving like a lunatic, party animal or anything else that would lead you down an undesirable road with a crazy outcome.

Spend time with friends who get your vision and want to support you on your journey. Real friends last a lifetime and do so because they're worth it!

THE BEST

No one loses out more than we do when we don't do our best. In doing your best, an example is set for those who follow. If something fails and you've tried hard and done the best you can do, there is no resonating feeling that you could have done more and didn't. You find strength; you pick up, move on and prepare to do the best for the next situation.

Performing at your highest level propels you spiritually and allows you to feel what reaching your highest potential is like.

Doing the best you can solidifies that you are a child of God.

POWER SUPPLY

We all have power. We all have our own personal reservoir of power and energy. How we choose to use our power is completely up to us. Many of us do not know how to use it while others are having it taken away. Several of us hate the thought of someone else having power and while some are too lazy to tap into their own, they would rather feed off another's.

Our power supply is bound to go dry if we do not acknowledge the source from which all power emits. The higher power gives us all we will ever need. God provides us with limitless power to achieve our goals and push us beyond what we ever thought we were capable of.

God is all.

POSITIVE THOUGHTS

Happiness is a state of mind

It all begins within the realm of your own head

Just like any invention or new found philosophy

It is all first created in the mind

Be careful of your thoughts
Mind over matter

To be in your right mind
Merely means to be in control of one's self

It is imperative that our thoughts remain Positive

Because anything else would be
A beautiful mind going to waste

INNOCENCE OF FRIENDSHIP

Real friends let you know when you're
stepping out of line
Friends are there to help if ever in a bind

Friends lend an ear because they do really
care

Friends are there to share in your laughter
Providing nothing but love and wanting
nothing thereafter

Through the pain, trials and tribulations
Friendship is golden is my estimation

If you give your heart you're sure to see
Just how rewarding a friendship can be

Through a great friend, God nurtures you

GOD IS LISTENING

How many times have you said,

"I wish I wouldn't have said that"

"If only I had bridled my tongue"

"If only I had chosen silence"

It's much easier to use those powerful words
To uplift, empower and praise

When you know that God is listening

LIVE LIFE

Tasting the bitter allows you to
appreciate the sweet
Cloudy days occur
So the sun is never taken for granted
Once in a while tears must roll
across our laugh lines
Most times death comes without
warning so that we may live each
and every day
To its highest potential
Express yourself
Be yourself
Stay true to you
Only take what you need and give all
that you've got
Nothing feels better than helping
someone
Turn a frown upside down

COURAGE

Having courage is a very splendid attribute to embark upon new challenges with knowing that all is well when accompanied by faith. There is never a fear when walking with the Almighty. Whether it's a move to a new location, new job or a new relationship, God loves it when we're humble, but He also loves when we're sure and courageous.

A SMILE

A smile can do a world of good. Smiling may teach us to feel good in a situation that would normally have us feeling negative and sad. A smile is a welcoming sign, letting others know that you believe in happiness and if things are not alright at the moment, they will certainly get better.

Smile a little more often and watch how it allows your heart to breathe.

HELP

To help another, in essence, is like helping oneself. Finding time in your busy schedule to help someone during a period of turmoil is extremely instrumental in knowing more about who you really are.

Instead of working so hard to avoid these types of situations, embrace helping someone who is near and dear to you. Although helping could mean financially, it also could mean a ride to the store, a hand with a task, or just simply providing an ear to listen. This is the time to open your heart; be kind and generous and expect that one day you too will be needing help.

WRONG DOINGS

We have all been and felt the pain of being wronged at sometime in our lives. But we also have acted as the perpetrator of these same acts with others. To forgive others is to forgive ourselves. Opening our hearts and choosing a positive way to deal with those who once upset us shows God we are willing.

If we expect God to forgive us, then we too should be expected to love and forgive our friends, family and peers.

MAKING IT

What does it take to make it? Depends on where you're going. The question is: are you prepared for the journey? Whatever the goal, you can be sure of one thing, it will take perseverance.

The intended goal will be met if you persevere. It will take courage in the face of all family, friends and foes who will tell you NO.

It will take discipline when every person, place or thing screams for your ATTENTION. It will take focus and determination, a will that goes beyond even your belief.

It will take FAITH in knowing you deserve everything GOOD that comes to you and knowing that anything negative is presented for your spiritual growth.

Now...are you ready for the ride of your life?!!

NO CHEATING

When you hold back and give less than what you really have, you'll never see the best results. No matter if it's a relationship, your job or your children. When you give less, that's exactly what you'll get in return. We cheat ourselves everyday by not expressing how we feel to the ones we love.

Sharing must come from all parties involved. Only then will the relationship reach its highest potential.

There is always a brighter side. Even when it seems like things can get worse. When you hit the bottom and negativity is holding you down like gravity, there is still a brighter side.

CREATE YOUR SPACE

Wherever you are, create your peace. Create that space within your own mind so that peace may lie there unbothered. There will always be times when you feel you're in the middle of chaos, when in actuality you are only where you allow yourself to be.

Escape mentally. Meditate in a quiet space and gain peace of mind.

SECRETS

Occasionally years and years of friendship sometimes can come to an unpleasant end. Does that mean years of trust, secrets and loyalty die as well? Certainly not. Your ex-friend's business should remain as private as the day it was shared with you. Loyalty is often abandoned when friendships dwindle, when marriages end, or when lovers become enemies. Always hold another's secrets dear to your heart as if they were your own. When someone shares their private world with you, it is a privilege. Respect their honesty and protect their privacy.

Treat others the way you want to be treated.

COMPLIMENTS

Compliments are not always easily received. We should allow others to admire us and share in their delight. Some find it extremely difficult to accept compliments, simply because we do not believe what is being said. However, beauty is in the eye of the beholder. Allow some of what they see to rub off on you so that finally you take note to all the beauty you possess inside and out.

Giving a compliment is beautiful, but also knowing how to graciously receive one is fantastic.

ACTION

Thoughts and inventions that manifest themselves into being are due to an individual focusing. Achieving your goals can be simple if there is a plan of hard work and action. You must focus on what must be done and literally stop at nothing until it is completed.

Your mind is capable of making all things real for you and with positive thinking and a tight plan, you can have all that you desire.

NEVER ASHAMED

We are all meant to learn from one another's mistakes, but how can we if no one admits having made any? Mistakes are a natural part of the learning process. If attention is paid to the experience, then it shouldn't have to be relived. Let's admit to our mistakes and allow our partners, kids and family to see that we are not ashamed to be wrong, but proud to work hard and do it correctly.

CHANCES

Have you any courage?
What happened to being
bold and adventurous?
What happened to taking
risks and gambling with
chances? Why play it safe
when none of us are
promised tomorrow? Go
after what makes your
heart beat faster and pumps
your adrenaline quicker.
Make an attempt at living
life (really).

Only when you take risks
will you find out what
you're really made of.

QUESTIONS

Never be afraid to ask questions. It gets mighty exhausting pretending to know everything. Inquire when you are uncertain or confused. In fact, don't hesitate to ask the same questions twice if you weren't satisfied with the first reply.

Asking questions may give you information you thought you knew but didn't. Asking questions also let's others know that you are open and willing to learn.

Ask, listen and learn.

PRESENT IS A PRESENT
The only time is here and now. The past and the future mean nothing if you won't make the best of here and now. Take in all that is now because it will never be the same; a moment will never be repeated. Enjoy your present moment.

Lavish being in this very second and create what it is that you want out of your life.

INCOMPARABLE PAIN

We sometimes believe people who come from the money side of the fence do not suffer hardships. Everyone has something to deal with and conquer. Your ordeal may appear worse because you're in it, but it doesn't necessarily mean it is. It is unfair to compare your pain to that of another because we all are living through this experience of life's ups and downs.

Handle your own and know that pain is pain and it really cannot be measured or compared.

MISDIRECTED AGGRESSION

Have you ever been annoyed with your life and let it affect how you treat others? The phone rings and you pick it up with an attitude. Someone knocks on the door and you answer with a less than pleasant well being.

One has nothing to do with the other. If you are having difficulties directing your aggression, you should take time out and breathe. Put yourself in those sets of circumstances and notice how undesirable that friend would be if they treated you meanly because of something else. Pick up the phone with a smile; someone called you, which means they really wanted to talk to you, or else they would've called someone else.

IT WILL HAPPEN

It is extremely easy to become frustrated when you line all your ducks up in a row and the plan doesn't pan out the way you wanted. Patience is a virtue and without it, we tend to jump before it's time. It is imperative that we keep the excitement and know and believe there is no possible way to stop before seeing that what you **WANT** to happen actually **DOES** happen.

YOUR INNER VOICE

Intuition is the mother of all and should not be ignored. That voice inside of your head speaks for no other reason but to inform you. That voice that says move quicker, don't go or speak up. That little voice that says I can do it all and accomplish very big things.

Listen and learn.

PLAYS CHANGE

No two people are alike. Never make someone suffer because of the wrong doings of another. No situation will ever present itself identically, so we must always be prepared to handle scenarios differently. Never assume it will play out like it did before.

It's a different play with different characters and a whole new script.

Approach it that way.

TIME WAITS NOT

Why does it seem there is never enough time to do all that we want and need to do? Why are we always running late and at the same time running out of time? Time moves and waits for no one; so why is it that sometimes it feels as if time is on our side? Well with knowing all this, the best thing to do is take full advantage of all your time and treat it preciously. Be grateful in the present, because the future is coming whether we worry about it or not.

WILL POWER

To have will power is to have faith that you will be blessed or rewarded by the unknown. To display will power is to not give in to temporary pleasures that do not fit within your future plans. To have will power is to use your better judgment when embarking upon new or old territory.

To openly share your struggles and weaknesses makes them real, which in turn, makes practicing discipline real.

Hold on to your beliefs and don't crumble under pressure.

SPIRITS FLY

Wouldn't it be great if we could have a travel agent book a flight, pack a bag and visit all our family and friends who have passed away? On the other hand, that might just be as painful as the day they moved on. Dealing with death can be extremely painful and even more so when it's unexpected. Although the circumstances may have been negative, we have to consider the transition from life to death as a passing from one realm to the next.

Death allows a spirit to fly and move on because it is no longer being held captive on earth.

HUGS WANTED

Do you ever wake up some mornings and just want a warm hug? Do you often get the desire to give a hug to someone in need? When wanting a hug, don't be ashamed. We all need that physical contact that comes from a pure place of love. A hug can send a beautiful message, with words never spoken. Next time you need a hug, don't hesitate to ask your mate, partner or dearest friend, or simply take your arms and wrap them around yourself.

Give a hug, it sends a signal of love and kindness.

PLANS MEAN NOTHING

Sometimes planning for something means absolutely nothing. You can schedule your life according to the things you'd like to do, but really your agenda means nothing. God moves us and puts us where He wants us to be, often times, to get a blessing or to avoid danger.

Never fight your instincts; that is God speaking and moving within you.

RAISE THE BAR

Every step you take should be towards excellence. Mediocrity should never be a resting zone for those who have big dreams. Dreams are necessary, but it's relentless focus and action that will call those beautiful images of success to manifest in this physical world.

Bringing your "A" game is what's going to be needed to aide in you being able to stand out from the rest. Your skill set must be up to par and your willingness to elevate beyond what is average will determine how much success can be attained.

Give your very best in all that you do. What you reap will be worth what you sow!!

INTUITION

Don't fight the time. There is a proper time and place for positive movement. Follow your God given intuition. Always trust your third eye and succumb to your spiritual self. Nothing occurs before its time and nothing thereafter. There is no better time than the present.

We should always be selective with how we spend our time, because not a second can be regained.

NEVER WAITING IN VAIN
Waiting for something that you want so desperately seems like waiting forever. Sometimes you want to give up in the middle of the storm. Other times, we shy away from what we want thinking if we finally got it, it might be disappointing. We must remember anything worth having is worth waiting for.

Stay busy in the interim, but never give up the dream or desire for what you want.

SHINE

Holding on to a grudge must be one of the most difficult things to do. It takes lots of work and energy to be anything less than loving towards others. It is much simpler to forgive and move on. That doesn't mean you forget it, it just means you do not allow the wrongdoings of others to sway you from being the ethically sound person that you have become.

Amongst the grime, you can still shine.

GUILT TRIP

How often do we inflict punishment on ourselves because of the past? It is gone, said and done. Hopefully a lesson was learned, but now it is time to keep it moving. Guilt is a powerful tool used by some to control others. However, it is ludicrous to put yourself through a guilt trip.

The trip is over.

WITHOUT TRUST

Trust is love in itself
Once bruised
Trusting is no easy task
However it is not impossible
Life's bumpy roads
Teach us to guard our inner most
thoughts and secrets
Close down the store front
Because the shop is shut down
But with no trust
There can be no open lines of
communication
Everyone is left to tip toe
No one states how they really feel
In fear of being judged by the other
Trust is essential
Trust is the heartbeat that allows
friendship to breath and live
Without trust, nothing at all can be
accomplished
Except an imaginary world of make
believe

MANY FACES

Today we spend so much valuable time hiding from others, that we actually lose sight of ourselves. Isn't it something when you forget about what you want, need and like? It's time to drop all the other faces you sometimes wear so that you may reveal you to you. Time to get familiar with you as a person and also what it is that can really fulfill you.

Let us stop pretending and get to the core of who we are.

DISCERNMENT

Patience is a virtue and certainly good things come to those who wait. Many times we feel as though we may have moved too fast with a situation not evaluating sufficiently. We should allow ourselves room for errors and then move on having learned from the ordeal. Patience allows you to see all for what it really is and people for who they really are. With patience comes discernment, which gives you clarity.

Be still and the answers will be given to you.

COMPANY IS GOOD

Because we lead very busy lives in the new millennium, sometimes it's great to stop, look and listen to the beauty that surrounds us. The sound of children's laughter, the sight of blooming flowers or a couple holding hands helps to make us feel alive. If you've ever imagined how it would be to live alone in the world, you quickly realize how much we need others to survive. It's a blessing to recognize that you can't do it alone and that sharing and opening your life to others is one of the most beautiful and healthy aspects of life.

RELEASE & LET GO

Letting go must be one of the most difficult tasks in life. When to walk away is a question we least want to ask ourselves; so in turn, while we ponder, waiting for the situation to get better or worse, we slowly let the love dwindle. Move into who you want to be by letting go of the past events that have somehow taken away who you really are.

Let go and face the challenges that will ultimately make you a better person.

DRUGS ARE NOT COOL

You think when you see a drug addict or alcoholic they were born that way? Most often, it was the inability to handle life. Many make the adjustments that need to be made while others fall victim to a temporary solution which turns out to be less of the solution they hoped for. In fact, using drugs to escape a problem ends up with the person not handling the original problem and then creating bigger problems.

Drugs leave you out of control of you and what goes on in your environment. Before you take any type of drug, ask someone who's willing to share the truth about their experience with drugs. Those who realize they have or had a problem will tell you it's not the road you ever want to venture down.

EVERYONE MAKES MISTAKES
Owning up to one's mistake can be almost impossible at times. It's even worse when you dig yourself into a debate and once you've realized you could be wrong, you still continue to argue.

Never fear admitting you were incorrect or a little off the mark. Everyone makes mistakes, but it's an intelligent person who can admit when they were wrong.

ADMISSION

Some of us will disagree until the cows come home. Others will debate as if it were an election to be won. Often times we go for so long that we forget what the original disagreement was about. Other times we're saying the same thing, just in a different way. And finally, once in a blue moon, we realize that we were wrong, but never have the courage to admit it. We should never be ashamed to admit a mistake. We all have made them and probably will in the future because no one is perfect, so why pretend to be?

Admit when you are wrong and move on.

GOSSIP

Gossip is contagious. He say . . . she say . . . what about what God say? We all at one point or another have fallen victim to making another a victim of verbal slander. We have to know that it isn't positive, healthy and it certainly isn't helpful to degrade and dehumanize another's character. Sometimes people talk about others to make themselves feel bigger when in fact, in God's eyes, we will always remain equal and filling ourselves with such nonsense and negativity can only result in ultimately feeling smaller.

Next time you feel the need to talk about someone offensively, stop and imagine them hearing you. Now it's not so much fun, huh?

DOING YOUR BEST

Living up to someone else's standards will never do. You can only display your best, and when that isn't enough, it has nothing to do with what you put forth. Some are not satisfied with themselves and in an attempt to fill the emptiness, they notice and speak of "so-called" short comings of others.

When you do and give your best, God allows those that matter to bear witness.

ACCEPTANCE

Acceptance from others means absolutely nothing if you won't accept yourself. We spend so much time seeking the approval of someone else that we forget to please ourselves. Coming to terms with not only accepting but learning to love everything about oneself is sometimes painful and difficult. Allowing God the space within our hearts to grow is the only way we will accept everything we once couldn't tolerate.

God is love, so let love rule. Stop judging yourself and know that the only one to please is God.

THE HIGH ROAD

It's so amazing how so many people love to take the easy road. For various reasons: too difficult, too lazy or they just don't recognize their own potential. Instead of exploring all options, we often grab at the first opportunity so that we can avoid the stress involved. However, we end up with stress anyway because we didn't take the time to really think the matter through, all options included. What's even more puzzling is when we make things harder than they have to be.

Drama is entertaining, but why go that route if instead peace can be maintained and your goal can be accomplished by taking the high road?

BLESSINGS

Making a commitment to your happiness should be a consistent way of living; however, we let every day rush us to an early death without ever reaching our goals. Your dreams can be fulfilled by simply applying yourself. Believe that it can be achieved. Aspirations come by way of God and if He gives you the vision, He will also bring it to pass.

Blessings sometimes sit dormant until you realize the power you have within to receive and use them.

JUDGE NOT

We all have fallen guilty to judging someone by their appearance. We look at their clothing and shoes quickly to give an evaluation and then treat them according to the box we put them in. How many times do you think you were judged before you opened your mouth to speak a word? Better yet, have you ever been looked at as if you were only worth as much as what you were wearing that day?

We should all learn to leave the judging up to God and be as loving and accepting as we would want others to be with us.

TRUTH WORKS

There is absolute power in truth. Nothing is more liberating than words that come from a place of honesty. Truth is the ingredient to a great way of living. When you expect truth, you give truth. Being able to always tell the truth involves trust. There are times when the fear of being judged can obscure your willingness to share the truth, when in fact, if you show all your cards, you will create relationships that are based on unconditional love.

LETTING GO

LETTING GO CAN SOMETIMES BE THE MOST DIFFICULT TASK TO ACCOMPLISH, BUT YET THE MOST REWARDING. LETTING GO OF OLD FRIENDSHIPS, PAST RELATIONSHIPS AND BAD HABITS CAN BECOME A TEDIOUS JOB.

WHEN PEOPLE AND SITUATIONS THAT WERE ONCE GOOD TURN SO BAD, IT IS TIME TO LEAVE AND MOVE ON. EXHALE THE OLD AND INHALE THE NEW.

LETTING GO AND ALLOWING GOD TO CHOOSE YOUR COMPANY IS THE BEST MOVE EVER.

TIMING

Often times we make an art of procrastination. Waiting to get things done rather than making things happen. But then there are also moments that are rushed, when no one enjoys waiting.

Finding a happy median is life's challenge. Learning when to move quickly with precision and knowing when to slow down and exercise patience are vital tools to succeeding in this game of life. Sometimes jumping the gun can get you burned and other times not moving quickly enough can get you left behind.

LIFE'S TRIP

If there is a will, there is a way. You should always know you have choices. Never feel as if you don't have an alternate move. You make choices every second of the day and whether you choose the positive path is up to you and you alone.

When coming to a crossroad, if confused, be sure to take your time with your decision. Most mistakes are made when you do not take a moment to think about the outcome. See it through and ask God to help you choose the best route for your life's trip.

EXPECTATION

Expectation is everything. It's the way you conduct yourself, the way in which you treat people, and the way you look at the world. Having faith concerning your happiness in the years to come is all based upon your positive outlook on the future.

Having great expectations allows your mind to see the vision, therefore bringing it into existence.

So shall a man thinketh . . . plan it, speak it, see it and it shall come to pass.

BEING UNIQUE

Having your own identity is certainly a task when everywhere in the media you are being persuaded to be like so many others. Establishing who you are and what you believe is imperative when aiming to be unique and original. Laying a foundation early before you are easily swayed is essential. Stick to your guns and don't allow the masses to have their way. Show the world you are truly one of a kind.

Everyone is born different, so why rush to catch up with the Jones' to become like everyone else?

THE COMPANY YOU KEEP
Know the company you keep or your company might keep you from reaching your highest potential.

It's important in life to spend as much time as possible with like-minded individuals: friends who understand your dreams and aspirations but also have desires of their own. Everyone in your circumference should be just as excited about life and their goals as you are, if not more.

Ask your friends, *"What are you most looking forward to?"* and *"What are your plans to attain the level of success you're after?"*

From the answers you're given you can assess whether you're in the right company.

FORGIVING

There have been moments when someone did something so disturbingly wrong to you it was beyond belief. You were probably angered and had no intentions of ever forgiving their actions. You may have gone as far as to put a revengeful plan of retaliation in motion. Know that you chose that experience and the lesson is all in the way you react. Never take it personal and always confront the perpetrator to let them know that you were deeply hurt by what they did.

Forgiving will allow your heart to remain open and your life will continue to grow.

GET LOVE

Giving love has to be one of the most natural processes of life. It's receiving love that becomes difficult. When you are not conditioned to receive love, it isn't easy to be told you're beautiful. It's hard to accept compliments and everyone is under suspicion. It is time to let go and absorb the love ready to reveal itself to you. Allow it to soak in and watch it create a glow from within. Being loved is very necessary to living a healthy life.

Open UP!!

UNDERSTANDING

Arguments exist because of differences in opinions. How sad would the world be if everyone thought the same thoughts? Varied opinions are necessary and vital to making the world colorful. To not accept an opinion because it differs from yours is like muting one of those glorious colors.

Before you argue another down, in hopes of having them abandon their idea to join your side, take a pause and understand that it's much more important to experience all the colors of the rainbow than it is to have a color missing because of your ego.

SUPPORT

You're playing yourself to give support to a person, place or thing without fully having an understanding of what "It" is your supporting. This includes your friends as well. Lending support takes time, energy and sometimes resources. You need to make sure all the support you're offering is going in the right places and is worthy of your efforts.

A lot of people choose to jump to the aide of another without understanding what they, themselves, may be entering into. Understand your moves before you make them.

NATURE

When was the last time you expressed your gratitude towards nature? The sun, the moon, the trees and every heavenly star that dances in the sky are all a part of the Creator's masterpiece. When was the last time you sat on a bench in a park, hiked up a mountain or ran down a boardwalk? Melting in the cascades of nature is free, so why not take full advantage of all that is available to help lift your spirits?

Your next day of relaxation should not be spent in front of the tv, but instead, in a park watching the birds and listening to God's creatures enjoying life as He made it.

MISTAKES

No one is perfect. Everyone makes mistakes. An error should be used as a lesson. Recognize what went wrong and then look to make things better. Lots of folks tend to beat themselves up when things don't go according to the plan that was first created. There is a reason for everything. Making a mistake does not make you a failure. Mishaps just season the personality, giving you more experience and a whole lot of flavor.

Learn from your mishaps so that maybe another will not have to walk in the same stretch.

KNOW YOURSELF

How are you feeling? What makes you feel the way you do? When do you feel that way? No matter how you've learned to deal in the world, it is still very important to understand your feelings. Your feelings, when investigated, can tell you so much about yourself. We spend a great amount of time attempting to hide our emotions so much so that we've hidden them very comfortably from ourselves! Our feelings are what bring us closer to knowing ourselves and becoming more in-tuned with others as well.

Whenever a situation, place or season evokes an emotion, notice how it makes you feel. Pause on everyone else and try to figure you out.

LISTEN

Talking is one thing but listening is a whole other thing in itself. To really hear is to have an open ear with no judgment. Listening is accepting. Listening is also sharing. Giving time to another is expected if a relationship is intended to grow and prosper. One of the greatest gifts one can give is the gift of allowing another to share with you, who they are.

Sure you have opinions, but once in a while, for the sake of knowing the other person better, take a moment and just listen.

THE VOICE WITHIN

Saying yes is usually an easy task. Saying no is what's most difficult. Maintaining a high level of self-discipline and self-respect is a goal certainly worth fulfilling. There have been times when you've gone against that inner voice of Godliness and the outcome left you feeling alone, shameful, and guilty. But, when you adhere to the God within you, it results in wise decisions that help you to maintain peace of mind.

Your happiness is most important and who can perform at their best with a guilty conscious?

CHANGE

Have you ever been so scared of change that you stayed away longer than you should have? Have you ever resented change because you really weren't ready? It is nearly impossible to hide from or outrun the inevitable, because change has got to come. Change is good and should be welcomed with open arms. If thought of in a positive manner, only great things can come from it. Most times, we fight change when it can actually be what's best for us. Loosen up and let nature have its way.

CONFIDENCE

Being bold and certain comes from knowing what you know. You can be clear about what you know when what you know is based on objective research and facts.

Gaining a bit of knowledge in all areas can be beneficial but really knowing what you may claim to be "your business" or "your gift" or "your talent" takes focus and intent. When studying for exams aim to REALLY know the information and not just from a memorization stand point.

Confidence comes from certainty and, when you're certain, it's because you KNOW.

RESPECT YOUR ELDERS

Whenever we speak to our elders it should be done with respect. Period, point blank!!

Too often young people behave disrespectfully towards the generation that laid the foundation prior to their arrival. It's time that kids, teens and young adults understand how important our parents, grandparents and elders are. Although we may not agree with how we were raised, we must know that honoring our elders comes with having grace and humility.

Most of all, you too will grow old and will look to those who are younger to honor your presence and treat you with the kindness you deserve.

HOLDIN' ON TOO LONG

Have you ever watched a film and became concerned for the well being of a fictitious character? The main character has grown and elevated to a newfound level that's promising and hopeful. Then along comes the friend from the past that has remained the same since grade school and shows no signs of ever mentally catching up. The film has hit a nerve.

Somewhere in life, we are faced with either holding on to a friendship that is no longer worth it or letting go of a friend whose season has passed. Either way, your life will be changed by what you choose to give attention to. Even when it hurts, it may be time to cut ties and say good-bye.

THE ROAD TO SUCCESS

There is one way to ensure success and that is the time and energy you put forth. Nothing is expected to happen if you do nothing. When you create a plan and figure a direction to head towards, you should never stop until you have arrived. There will be many detours and distractions along the way that pose happiness, but they will all be temporary. They will reveal themselves in time as being insufficient and before long, you will be back on the road in an attempt to reach those long term goals again.

Stay focused. When you go astray, do not beat yourself up, but recognize it and step back into the divine plan.

THE BEAUTIFUL MIND

Only with memories can we hold on to the relationships we have built with others. With past experiences that are shared comes an invisible common bond. On the other hand, the imagination is where ideas are created and your future is made. The mind is such a powerful tool used to create and modify your life and surroundings.

Think BIG!

LOVE YOURSELF

It's time we start treating ourselves like some of the people we love. We give attention, we spend time and we listen. Now, do all of that for you.

Treat YOU like you mean something. That's what self-love is all about. It's hard for anyone to mistreat you when you know how you like to be treated. Let others meet up to the standards for what is acceptable treatment towards you.

Don't' mistreat yourself: eat right, exercise, stay aware. No one is going to look out for you the way you do for yourself.

YOUR WORD

The older you get the more you experience. The wiser you become the more you realize . . . all we have are words. When we have nothing else to share we have words to lend to another. Promises are so easily broken in a time when promises are made every day. I've come to know that words are an extension of the soul and when making a promise, the best that can ever be done is keeping it.

In a world where everything can change in a second's time, keeping your word is divine.

UNSTOPPABLE

There are moments when hardships occur and times when you may be led to believe you should give up – that possibly all you've dreamed of is just one huge "Pie in the sky" and will be forever unattainable. Feelings of inadequacy begin to fester and all that could deter you from your goals seem to appear: full blown and in living color.

Here you stand at a crossroad with your future depending on you to either continue with your mission or retreat because of a few failures. Those who choose to retreat and have done it successfully weren't meant for the wins God had intended for them. But you are different. You are unstoppable because you are strong. The strong survive no matter the adversities, knowing that challenges along the way prove they are undoubtedly blazing new trails.

GET MOVIN'

Wait for no one! Get it movin'! Make it happen! Go for the gusto. Take on the world. Only you can change the course of your life. You have the control to either sit or stand. You have the power to overcome adversities and make successes out of nothing.

Good luck and may God bless you on your journey.

Join the Movement:
www.hiphopsistersnetwork.org

About Hip-Hop Sisters Network
Founded by MC Lyte, the legendary lyricist and iconic hip-hop pioneer, Hip Hop Sisters Network is a non-profit organization that promotes positive images of women of ethnic diversity, bringing leaders from the world of Hip Hop, the entertainment industry, and the corporate world.

HHSN provides national and international support to women and youth around the globe on the topics of:

Cultural Issues;

Financial Empowerment;

Health and Wellness;

Mentorship; and

Educational Opportunities.

Celebrity advisory board members include Faith Evans, Ledisi, Jada Pinkett Smith, Chilli, Russell Simmons, Cheryl "Salt" James, Malinda Williams, Kelly Price, Malcolm Jamal Warner, and Dr. Benjamin Chavis.

Hip Hop Sisters Network welcomes and embraces partnership opportunities with individuals and institutions that contribute to the empowerment of people across the globe.

About MC Lyte

Lyricist, pioneer, icon, inspirational speaker, veteran and entrepreneur describe one of the most prolific and well-respected female Hip Hop artists of our time: **Lana "MC Lyte" Moorer**. A pioneer in the industry, she opened the door for future female Hip Hop artists by daring to do what had never been done while doing something she loved. A role model to women and respected by men everywhere, Lyte never compromises who she is and consistently displays that a woman can turn heads fully clothed!

Whenever possible, **Lyte,** as she is affectionately known by her inner circle, enjoys traveling across the nation to use her expertise and story of success to motivate others to take ownership of the world around them while striving to be the best they can possibly be.

Author of "**Unstoppable: Igniting the Power Within to Achieve Your Greatest Potential**," **MC Lyte** is also very active in many social projects, including anti-violence campaigns and Rock the Vote.

MC Lyte is the presiding President of the Los Angeles Chapter of the Recording Academy and she is also a proud honorary member of Sigma Gamma Rho Sorority, Inc.